Javeed the Magician

Written by Rufus Baker

Illustrated by Wendy Tan Shiau Wei

Javeed was in hospital. He'd had an operation, and he was looking forward to going home soon.

It will be great to sleep in my own bed again, he thought.

"Javeed, do you want to come and watch Faiz the Fantastic?" asked one of the nurses. "He's come to cheer us all up this morning!"

"A magician? Boring!" mumbled Javeed.

Javeed and all the other children watched as Faiz the Fantastic swept into the ward. He was dressed in a tall, black hat and a long cloak.

"Behold my special box!" the magician said.

Javeed thought the box just looked like his wardrobe at home.

"I will make whoever steps inside this box vanish!" Faiz cried.

Everyone gasped.

Faiz asked Javeed's friend, Olivia, to step into the box.

"BISH, BIP, BOOGLE, BANISH!" roared Faiz, and he flung the door back.

Olivia had vanished!
Even Javeed was shocked.

"Watch," Faiz said. "When I flick my wand, Olivia will return!"

Faiz waved his wand, flung the door back again, and Olivia wandered forward.

That night, Javeed had an amazing dream. His name was Javeed the Magician, and he was standing on a stage wearing a long, blue cloak and a tall hat.

Everyone in the crowd watched and cheered as he performed clever tricks and illusions, just like Faiz the Fantastic.

The next morning, Javeed's parents took him home. He talked about Faiz the Fantastic all the way back.

"Faiz teaches people how to perform tricks, too," Javeed said. "Can I go to one of his lessons? I'd be a great magician!"

"You wanted to be a musician last week!" Dad laughed. "But yes, why not?"

Mum gave Javeed permission to go to the workshop, too.

"Will you put on a show for us afterwards?" she asked.

"Of course!" Javeed grinned as he gave his parents a hug.

The day of the workshop arrived. Javeed was glad to see some of his new friends from the hospital ward were there, too.

During the workshop session, Javeed learned all kinds of tricks.

He made a spoon bend in half …

… and made a gold coin appear from behind Dan's ear.

He made flowers pop up from nowhere without warning, a ball float in the air and water vanish from a jug and turn into glitter.

Before he went home, Javeed wanted to see the special box again.

"Could I have a go at the vanishing trick, please?" he asked.

"I normally keep this illusion top secret!" said Faiz. "But just this once, I'll share it with you. Get into position, and I'll show you how to do it."

Faiz whispered the instructions for the illusion into Javeed's ear.

"Aha!" grinned Javeed.

Javeed could not wait to put on the special show he had promised his mum. She had invited all their friends and family for the occasion!

Javeed had never seen so many people in his house all at once! He showed them all the tricks he knew, and they cheered, laughed and clapped.

Then it was time for the big finish!

"Sana!" he called to his sister. "Would you like to step into this special wardrobe?"

Sana's eyes were wide with excitement. She stepped inside and Javeed waved his wand.

"You didn't mention that your sister would disappear!" gasped Mum. "Where is she?"

"I'm here, Mum!" Sana popped out of the wardrobe again. The audience clapped and cheered.

"You really are a magician!" said Mum.

"Remember when you thought magicians were boring, Javeed?" said Dad.

"No way. Magicians are the best!" giggled Javeed.

Phonics Practice

Say the sound and read the words.

/o/	(w)a

watch   wand   swan   want   washing
wasps   wander

/sh/	-ssi

mission   session   permission
passion   admission

/sh/	-ci

special   official   artificial   optician
musician   magician

Can you say your own sentences using some of the words on these pages?

What other words do you know that are spelled in these ways?

/sh/	-ti

station   position   mention   motion
direction   correction

Common exception words

called   asked   could   water
where   who

We may say some words differently because of our accent.

Talk about the story

Answer the questions:

1 Why did Faiz the Fantastic visit the hospital?

2 What did Javeed agree he would do after he had been to the illusion workshop?

3 Why do you think Faiz the Fantastic whispered the instructions for the vanishing trick to Javeed?

4 Why did Mum gasp during Javeed's show?

5 Have you ever seen someone perform illusions like Faiz the Fantastic? What did they do?

6 What special skills would you like to learn?

Can you retell the story in your own words?